The Infamous Rapture Conflict

Rev. Terry Lee Miller, SR.

Xulon
PRESS

PREFACE

The Doctrinal Position of This Book

It needs to be stated that this book re-establishes the historic doctrinal position the church held for 1800 years of church history concerning the timing of the rapture, and catching up of the Saints, at the return of Jesus.

This book, however, according to theological interpretation by the three camps, pre-post and mid-trib rapturists, is to them of a Mid-trib rapture position, but according to the Scriptures when rightly divided it is a:

POST TRIB DOCTRINAL EXPOSITION
IN TRUTH AND STAND COMPLETELY
SUPPORTED BY THE WORD OF GOD.

Simply spoken, the church would undergo severe trials and persecutions culminating with the appearance of the Antichrist and his attacks upon the church. Then Jesus would come back, rapture His saints, bring judgement on the earth, and set His kingdom upon the earth for a thousand years of peace. A probable reason for confusion and hair splitting in these end days is that the last 100 years or so we have moved into a very technical, scientifically organized society demanding accuracy and clarity in our doctrinal positions. This is perhaps good except that the average Christian is unable to sort out these confusing and contradicting doctrinal positions.

It is our prayer that this book will erase these differences and bring all three schools of thought into agreement.

BIBLICAL TRUTHS RE-ESTABLISHED BY THIS BOOK AFTER NEARLY 200 YEARS OF PRE-TRIB HERESY

For 1800 years of church history the following truth was held by the New Testament church: The church would undergo trials and afflictions while carrying out her mission on earth to preach the gospel to all nations. That mission would culminate with the appearance of the man of sin who would attack and try to destroy the people of God. He would then come to power and reign briefly over the entire earth. Then the Lord would come and gather out His people and bring the judgements of Revelation on the earth, thus beginning the period prophesied in the Old Testament called the Day of the Lord. This time is signed with cosmic disturbances. At the end of the wrathful judgements on earth Christ would return with his saints to fight the Battle of Armageddon, bringing in the millennium.

This simple truth was held for 1800 years of church history, and this exact truth is what this book re-establishes in scriptural definitiveness. (Dave McPherson's book on "Rapture" proves this point with more than adequate documentation)!

Barnabas (40-100)
The final stumbling block (or source of danger) approaches...for the whole [past] time of your faith will profit you nothing, unless now in this wicked time we also withstand coming sources of danger...That the Black One [Antichrist] may find no means of entrance...

(Epistle of Barnabas, 4)

Clement of Rome (40-100)
...the Scripture also bears witness, saying, "Speedily will He come, and will not tarry;" and, "The Lord shall suddenly come to His temple, even the Holy One, for whom ye look."

(I Clement, 23)

Tertullian (150-200)
The souls of the martyrs are taught to wait...that the beast Antichrist with his false prophets may wage war on the Church of God...

(On the Resurrection of the Flesh, 25)

Cyril of Jerusalem (315-386)
The Church declares to thee the things concerning Antichrist before they arrive...it is well that, knowing these things, thou shouldest make thyself ready beforehand.

(Catechetical Lectures, 15, 9)

Augustine (354-430)
But he who reads this passage [Daniel 12], even half asleep, cannot fail to see that the kingdom of Antichrist shall fiercely, though for a short time, assail the Church...

(The City of God, XX, 23)

Venerable Bede (673-735)
[The Church's triumph will] follow the reign of the Antichrist...

(The Explanation of the Apocalypse, II, 8)

John Wycliffe (1320-1384)
Wherefore let us pray to God that he keeps us in the hour of temptation, which is coming upon all the world, Rev. iii...
(Writings of the Reverend and Learned John Wickliff, D.D., 155)

Martin Luther (1483-1546)
[The book of Revelation] is intended as a revelation of things that are to happen in the future, and especially of tribulations and disasters for the Church...
(Works of Martin Luther, VI, 481)

John Bunyan (1628-1688)
He comes in flaming fire [as Judge] and...the trump of God sounds in the air, the dead to hear his voice...
(The Four Last Things: Of Judgement)

John Wesley (1703-1791)
"The stars shall...fall from heaven," (Revelation, vi., 13)...And then shall be heard the universal shout...followed by the 'voice of the archangel'...'and the trumpet of God'...(I Thessalonians iv., 16).
(The Works of the Rev. John Wesley, A.M., V, 173)

John Newton (1725-1807)
'Fear not temptation's fiery day, for I will be thy strength and stay. Thou hast my promise, hold it fast, the trying hour [Revelation 3:10] will soon be past.'
(The Works of Rev. John Newton, II, 152)

Charles Finney (1792-1875)
Christ represents it as impossible to deceive the elect. Matt. 24:24. We have seen that the elect unto salvation includes all true Christians.
(Lectures on Systematic Theology, 606)

George Mueller (1805-1898)
The Scripture declares plainly that the Lord Jesus will not come until the Apostasy shall have taken place, and the man of sin...shall have been revealed..
(Mrs. Mueller's Missionary Tours and Labours, 148)

Oswald T. Allis (1880-1973)
...the 'any moment' doctrine of the coming owes its popularity to a desire to escape the evils which are to come upon all the earth...
(Prophecy and the Church, 208)

Oswald J. Smith

...I am absolutely convinced that there will be no rapture before the Tribulation, but that the Church will undoubtedly be called upon to face the Antichrist...

(Tribulation or Rapture -- Which?, 2)

Loraine Boettner
Hence we conclude that nowhere in Scripture does it teach a secret or pretribulation Rapture...

(The Millennium, 168)

George Ladd
[Pre-Tribulationism] may be guilty of the positive danger of leaving the Church unprepared for tribulation when Antichrist appears...

(Worthy is the Lamb, 123)

Dale Moody
There is not a passage in the New Testament to support Scofield. The call to John to 'come up hither' has reference to mystical ecstasy, not to a pretribulation rapture.

(Spirit of the Living God, 203)

This book shows that:

1. The pre-tribists imminent, secret rapture doctrine is established by: a) wresting of scriptures out of context, b) misapplication of scriptures, c) misinterpretation of scriptures, d) promising the church deliverance from the Antichrist. This false doctrine cannot trace its roots back much before the 1800s if that.

2. The post-trib rapture position <u>as defined by the three camps</u> is a false position though the scriptures <u>do</u> teach a post-trib rapture, but only when the scriptures are rightly divided as they were for 1800 years of church history.

3. Our Savior taught a post-trib rapture.

4. The mid-trib rapture as defined by the three camps is basically correct except that the terminology must be changed to be scriptural.

5. There is no such scriptural definition of a seven year tribulation.

6. The tribulation period is not seven years, but rather is approximately

2,000 ± years from the destruction of Jerusalem under the prototype Antichrist Titus through the final Antichrist and his persecutions of the church. This ends at the 6th seal and cosmic disturbances, rapture and return of Christ. (Leaving 3-1/2 years of wrath on earth beginning the vengeful Day of the Lord until Christ's Revelation.

7. The secret, imminent (any second) pre-Daniel's 70th week rapture simply does not exist in scripture.

8. The first 3-1/2 years of Daniel's 70th week, yet unfilled, is the last 3-1/2 years of the 2000 ± years of tribulation or affliction of the church (prophesied by Jesus which lasts the entire N.T. church age and ends with the rapture.)

9. The last 3-1/2 years of Daniel's 70th week is the first 3-1/2 years of the Day of the Lord. This begins with the rapture and then proceeds with the unparalleled wrath of God in the seventh seal, seven trumpets, and seven vials to subdue the earth including the millennium age and ending with the renovation by fire of the heavens and earth.

10. The pre-trib imminent rapture position is false, totally unscriptural and is shown irrefutably to its true origin by world renown biblical researcher, Dave MacPherson. His newest book, "The Rapture Plot," completely puts to rest any question as to the origin of this latter day heresy.

   Order from: Millennium III Publishers
           P.O. Box 928
           Simpsonville, SC 29681
           Price: $14.95 plus $1.50 shipping & handling
           Or call: 1-(800) 967-7345 to order

11. The scriptures do teach an imminent return of Christ, not a pre-trib but a post-trib imminent return.

Table of Contents

Chapter 1

My Personal Testimony Concerning
Conversion From The Pre-Trib Rapture Position

As a new convert in 1961, I was immediately schooled in Pre-trib rapture doctrine by a godly Christian worker, E. Manning of Memphis Tennessee, who also brought me to Christ, and then by Baptist Bible College (1963-67) located in Springfield, Missouri. This I vigorously defended for about 25 years. As time went along, I became very concerned about seemingly contradictions in scriptures, but since we who love Holy Writ know that contradictions can not be with God's word but rather with our understanding of it, I was determined by God's grace to resolve the differences. I would discuss these problems with any person who seemed to be a mature student of God's word. I began wrestling with this problem in 1970. The problem was the cosmic disturbances of Matt. 24:29 which were "immediately after the tribulation..." of Daniel's 70th week. These disturbances which announced Christ's return in glory, seemed to contradict Rev. chapter 6 when identical disturbances came after the sixth seal, followed by the trumpets and vial judgements which must have lasted up to 3-1/2 years or longer. The term "Immediately after the tribulation of those days..." in my thinking was dogmatically, absolutely, and irrefutably simply stating, "Immediately after Daniel's 70th week." From this faulty foundation I would attempt to unravel the book of Revelation. The simple fact is, I could not because my foundation was faulty indeed.

Four irrefutable facts which pre-tribists unconsciously overlook are first, that the Day of the Lord, the return of Christ to judge and subdue the world, is announced by special cosmic disturbances. For example, the sun is darkened and the moon is turned to blood -- events that never have happened before, nor ever will happen again. These two simultaneous cosmic displays, and these alone, announce the final return of Jesus. This cannot be refuted. Second, these cosmic disturbances happen only once, immediately prior to the return of Christ in judgement. (Verse 10 plainly shows the rapture occurs when He comes to be glorified in His saints. This will be at Christ's coming to bring vengeance on the wicked in verse 8). The third is that all of the redeemed will be removed from this earth before the vengeance of Christ is poured out during this time which is called the Day of the Lord. The Day of the Lord begins with these special cosmic signs and ends when the heavens are renovated by fire. [See II Pet. 3:7-13]. That the redeemed are removed from this earth before the vengeance of God falls is plainly seen in [II Thess. 1:6-10] verse 8, compared to [I Thess. 4:14-5:10]. The vengeful Day of the Lord in 5:2-3 is portrayed as happening as soon as the rapture takes place. See I Thess. 4:15-18 and continue reading through I Thess. 5:10.

The cosmic disturbances, therefore, become a central pivotal point in the arena of prophecy. (Since my foundation was built upon the false idea that "immediately after the tribulation" was saying "immediately after Daniel's 70th week," quite naturally I termed the gathering to be a gathering of the Jews from the four corners of the earth and the judgement of the nations at the end of Daniel's 70th week, to be the same, and thus making the "elect" the Jewish elect. The fourth is that the scriptures do not say nor imply "immediately after Daniel's 70th week." To say differently is to add a forced interpretation leading to a faulty conclusion.

[The faulty interpretation by both pre- and post-tribists is through a very superficial reading of this important passage and taking it out of its context. Before I get away from the original message of this section, back to my personal testimony.]

In 1967 after graduation, I drove through Toronto, Canada to attend the famous People's Church pastored by the world renowned Dr. Oswald J. Smith. Upon meeting him and expressing my deepest appreciation for his wonderful books and missionary vision, (Dr. Smith has written over 1,200 Christian hymns and songs as well; his church was supporting over 200 missionary families full time), I must say how dare people like Tim LaHaye charge mid- and post-trib believers with diminishing one's love and eager expectation for our Lord's return. Dr. Smith and people like him have probably done far more in evangelism and song writing than any other man alive, even though he did hold the modern post-trib position. He gave me several books, one of which was from England, "Our Lord Returneth" by Mr. Rowlands. Upon reading the book later, most of the current post-trib (post-Daniel 70th week rapture) views were easily discarded except for his comments on II Thess. 2:7 which totally repudiated my faulty doctrinal position on the removal of the Holy Spirit along with the church when rendered in its literal sense in the Greek: "EK MESOU GENETAI" i.e., "OUT OF THE MIDST COMES TO BE." The word "taken" does not exist in the Greek: (This cannot be refuted, see and compare Strong's). The import of this verse literally is that the restrainer will restrain until the Antichrist arises out of the midst of lawlessness. (See fuller explanation in chart). Just why this verse was translated "taken" was a total mystery to me until I finally discovered that the first English translation ever (Wycliff in the 1300s) translated it this way and the reformers and all other translators since were evidently faithful to his translation. Antiquity was a

The Infamous Conflict
1

determining factor for its reproduction even though it was an unclear translation. Wycliff did not mistranslate the verse, but rather he had to take a difficult verse and translate it to English. Naturally the obscure meaning followed: The pre-tribists are notorious with using an English word not represented in Greek to build a removal of the church doctrine, even to the point of breaking fellowship. If any one is guilty, they are by adding a doctrine where it is impossible to support it in the Greek.

To simply say that the Holy Spirit returns to heaven and works on the earth as He did in the Old Testament and before the day of Pentecost, is simply and purely a matter of forced, fabricated interpretation plainly adding a theological doctrine to a verse of scripture where it does not exist in the Greek. [I have become convinced that the Ruckmanite movement has been a Satanic tool to attempt to repudiate any reliability in the Greek and Hebrew manuscripts.

The Ruckmanite movement is headed by the notorious apostate Peter Ruckman, who pastors and heads a Bible Institute in Pensacola, Florida. To those who say I should not label and name people, I say read Romans 16:17; also remember they have caused themselves to be labeled by their own false doctrines. For those who have not followed the evolution of Ruckmanism, Dr. Ruckman is the first person in all of church history to claim 1) a translation (K.J.V.) is superior to the texts from which it was taken, 2) that the 1611 K.J.V. contains over 20 advanced new revelations which did not exist in the manuscripts from which they were taken, 3) that the K.J.V. 1611 with the English dictionary can correct any Greek/Hebrew manuscript in existence, 4) he considers all of those who disagree with him on these points to be in apostasy. Absolutely no one, to my knowledge, in all of church history has ever held this theory; and amazing as it may seem he has quite a following, 5) he claims that the 1611 K.J.V. is a letter perfect, infallibly perfect translation of the original languages, absolutely flawlessly superintended by the Holy Ghost (even the italicized words) -- not even the translators claimed this! Ruckman thus is setting himself up as God by claiming advanced revelations.

It is a simple historical fact the translators never claimed infallibility and also a fact that the underlying Greek/Hebrew text of the K.J.V. can further clarify the few, obscure, difficult passages by Greek word studies that do exist in the English translation. Lest one reading this misunderstand, perhaps it should be stated that the K.J.V. does a perfect work in conveying the saving gospel of our Lord Jesus Christ as well as to clearly give all of us our biblical doctrines called pillars of the faith. The K.J.V. is a wonderful and beautiful translation of God's word. Where obscurities or uncertainties arise in any area of Christian theology, the student of God's word must tread lightly and with love. I use the 1611 K.J.V. along with the original languages.

Getting back to my story of trib conversion with Mr. Rowland's Greek exposition on II Thess. 2:7 paving the way to my present stand. This point came in the mid to late 80s, through many hours of studies, that I finally came to see that the rapture would be post-trib (only after the first 3-1/2 years being the trib of "those days") and pre-wrath (before the last 3-1/2 years of Daniel's 70th week). I need to add here that I have come to see the rapture, note carefully here, taking place shortly after the opening of the sixth seal, some time in the midst or <u>approximately</u> the middle of Daniel's 70th week. This approximation is scriptural since no man knows the day nor the hour of the coming of our Savior.

Being convinced of the truth of my new doctrinal position, I was reluctant to take an open stand on it, realizing that I am but a sinner saved by grace and still fallible. If there was the remotest possibility that I was wrong I certainly needed to know. I did not want to teach heresy in ignorance! I began going about discussing it with anyone possible but few, if any, wanted to discuss it; and if they did they would only present several verses of scriptures almost irrelevant to the subject. I would also shy away from taking a stand because the pre-tribists were nearly equating the mid-trib rapture position with a denial of the return of Jesus. They also were falsely charging, with a subtle play on words, that anyone outside the pre-trib camp was really looking for the coming of Antichrist rather than the coming of our Lord. This is as ridiculous to say as it would be to say the wise men were really looking for the star of David rather than the first coming of Christ.

Shortly after my conversion to mid-trib rapture position, I found Marvin Rosenthal's book and upon reading it I found that I generally agreed with the main import of it, post-trib pre-wrath position. The point I could not accept was the placing of the rapture sometime late in the last portion of the 70th week of Daniel (last 3-1/2 years). I am able to honestly say that I have arrived at my present position through: 1) using a literal interpretation of God's word except when the context demands a figurative one, 2) drawing a large chart of Daniel's 70th week and placing on it events of the scripture in the order that they appear in the scriptures.(Naturally not minimizing meditation and prayer) Finally arriving at a mid-trib, (post-trib, pre-wrath position), I was very sure that I had no further to go in my long quest for a reconciliation of very difficult scriptures. However, I had one more step to go.

Chapter II

One Final Step

Upon meditating on the term "tribulation <u>OF THOSE DAYS</u>" (Matt. 24) and reading and re-reading the entire context preceding back to the disciples basic questions, (i.e. "What shall be the sign of thy coming? When shall these things be? The sign of the end of the world?"), and also remembering that Mark 13:19&24 uses the word affliction instead of tribulation. It suddenly dawned on me that Jesus was giving his disciples exactly the answer they wanted, namely an entire, descriptive panoramic vision of the entire New Testament church age from the destruction of Jerusalem down to the final appearance of the Antichrist and to Jesus' final coming which was to be immediately preceded by the cosmic signs.

When He said "Immediately after the tribulation (or afflictions) of THOSE DAYS" he meant just that, the days from the destruction of Jerusalem up until the cosmic disturbances announcing His return for the church - approximately 2000 years of affliction and trial on the people of God. Plainly the N.T. church age ends at the sixth seal and the cosmic disturbances of the sun turning black and the moon to blood. The light suddenly broke on my soul that there was <u>no such period</u> as a seven year "tribulation" but rather an approximately 2,000 year tribulation ending at the sixth seal. This would mean that the first 3-1/2 years of Daniel's 70th week is really only the tail end of the long period of trials and afflictions appointed to the church, culminating with the appearance and persecution of Antichrist upon the church (during the time period indicated as, "For then shall there be great tribulation" and with Christ's return at the sixth seal/cosmic disturbances/rapture and beginning of the vengeful Day of the Lord!

Also, I saw that my position as a mid-trib was in reality a position unscripturally defined by the pre-trib camp. According to the scriptural definition of things, I was really a post-trib rapturist now. (Post N.T. church age - exactly what the church held for 1800 years of church history!)

Matt. 24 has been wrongly divided for years and years by Bible teachers though I suppose through ignorance. Our Savior was outlining the entire N.T. church age in all of its afflictions, persecutions, and trials from the destruction of Jerusalem in 70 A.D., this including all of the Diocletions, Neros, Popes, Emperors, inquisitions and Foxes Book of Martyrs heroes of the faith.

Finally, the infamously celebrated mystery of iniquity comes to its supreme development, and is revealed in the supreme Antichrist who will make one last and final effort to blot out every vestige of Biblical Christendom on earth by slaughtering millions and millions of truly born-again believers (while they are futily awaiting a false pre-Daniel's 70th week rapture).

Pre-tribbers enjoy the financial gain of being popular with main stream fundamentalism which is thoroughly cancered with the pre-70th week of Daniel's rapture heresy. (It is well to add here that even if Daniel's 70th week was historically fulfilled, there is ample proof in Revelation that the period of time from the opening of the first seal until Christ returns at the end of Revelation with His saints is seven years in length, with the rapture occurring approximately in the midst (middle) of the week at the sixth seal!)

Popular, yes.   True, no!   The apostle Paul was so concerned that Christians needed to realize the Day of the Lord and our gathering unto Him (rapture) was not imminent (at any moment) that he plainly said that they were not to be deceived by any means for that day, the Day of Christ, would not come until there was FIRST a falling away (apostasy) and that man of sin be revealed. This apostasy can be easily seen by Dr. Jack Van Impe who for years was a staunch defender of fundamentalism. Recently, he came out on nationwide TV stating that the five fundamentals or pillars of the faith were all that one needed to believe to be termed a "child of God." The five pillars of the faith as follows: 1) Virgin birth of Christ, 2) Inspiration of the Scriptures, 3) Bodily resurrection of Christ, 4) Deity of Christ, and 5) Blood atonement of Christ.

If this is true then every demon this side of perdition is a son of God because they believe and tremble. Not only they, but every unregenerate church member who believes the five pillars of the faith but has not yet had a born-again experience is also a child of God! This is heresy and apostasy coming out in its final form. Mr. Van Impe also has given his basic stamp of doctrinal approval to the Roman Catholic Church Catechism (I believe published in 1994 - the most recent) which is full of heresy. The demons of hell must be truly rejoicing in his conversion from main stream fundamentalism to main stream apostasy. [The simple fact is that I have written to him several times warning him of his apostasy but to no avail.] Following is a doctrinal statement on the plan of salvation I put together and sent him.

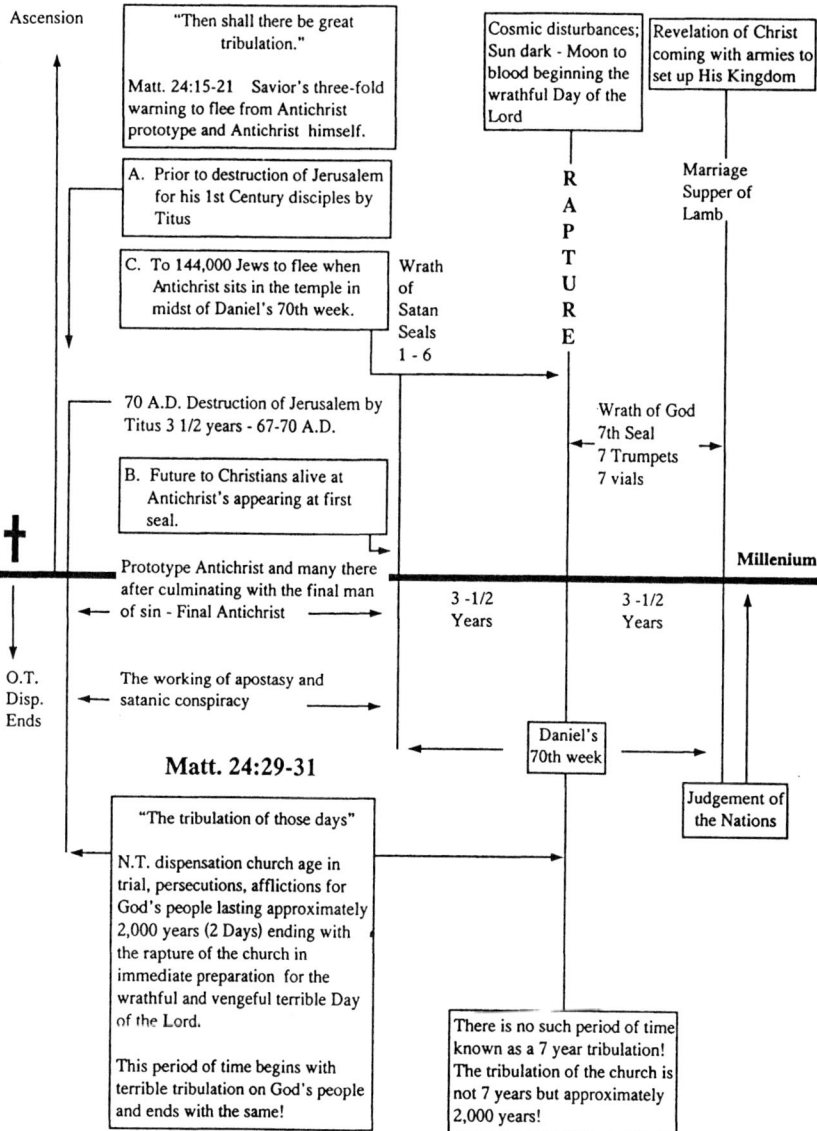

Matt. 24:21

Ascension

"Then shall there be great
tribulation."

Matt. 24:15-21 Savior's three-fold
warning to flee from Antichrist
prototype and Antichrist himself.

Cosmic disturbances;
Sun dark - Moon to
blood beginning the
wrathful Day of the
Lord

Revelation of Christ
coming with armies to
set up His Kingdom

A. Prior to destruction of Jerusalem
for his 1st Century disciples by
Titus

R
A
P
T
U
R
E

Marriage
Supper of
Lamb

C. To 144,000 Jews to flee when
Antichrist sits in the temple in
midst of Daniel's 70th week.

Wrath
of
Satan
Seals
1 - 6

70 A.D. Destruction of Jerusalem by
Titus 3 1/2 years - 67-70 A.D.

Wrath of God
7th Seal
7 Trumpets
7 vials

B. Future to Christians alive at
Antichrist's appearing at first
seal.

Millenium

Prototype Antichrist and many there
after culminating with the final man
of sin - Final Antichrist

3 -1/2
Years

3 -1/2
Years

O.T.
Disp.
Ends

The working of apostasy and
satanic conspiracy

Matt. 24:29-31

Daniel's
70th week

Judgement of
the Nations

"The tribulation of those days"

N.T. dispensation church age in
trial, persecutions, afflictions for
God's people lasting approximately
2,000 years (2 Days) ending with
the rapture of the church in
immediate preparation for the
wrathful and vengeful terrible Day
of the Lord.

This period of time begins with
terrible tribulation on God's people
and ends with the same!

There is no such period of time
known as a 7 year tribulation!
The tribulation of the church is
not 7 years but approximately
2,000 years!

Doctrinal Statement On The Only Way of Salvation

Salvation is the immediate attainment of complete deliverance from the penalty of sin in its entire scope, and that by the new birth and the new birth alone, it cannot be added to nor taken from. First, the method of salvation must be absolute in its doctrinal message. Second, the method must be absolute in its effect. God cannot be immutable nor without falsehood if salvation has more than one plan of attainment. Simply stated, salvation is an unconditionally free gift purchased and paid for with the blood of Christ and is attained only by repentance of sin and exercised faith in Jesus Christ as God and Savior. Furthermore, salvation must be received without a view or effort toward personal merit or holiness as a means of help in attainment, no matter how small the effort may be.

Herein lies the difference between the true gospel of salvation and the false satanically inspired gospels such as that of the Roman Catholic Church. Satanically inspired gospels or ways of salvation taint the faith of those followers; and in so doing, close up the door of salvation to them. This tainted faith is not fully persuaded, which is an absolute necessary prerequisite to being qualified for salvation. Romans 4:20-25, "He staggered not at the promise of God through unbelief; but was strong in faith, giving glory to God; And being fully persuaded that, what he had promised, he was able also to perform. And therefore it was imputed to him for righteousness. Now it was not written for his sake alone, that it was imputed to him; But for us also, to whom it shall be imputed, if we believe on Him that raised up Jesus our Lord from the dead; Who was delivered for our offenses, and was raised again for our justification." (It needs to be added here - Where in church history have non-Catholic Christians <u>ever</u> put Catholics to death, sword, stake, torture and inquisitions? Never! But Roman Catholicism has a bloody past in slaughtering multitudes of non-Catholic Christians over the centuries. Ever any official apology? <u>Never</u>! The Catholic Church claims infallibility! See Foxes Book of Martyrs!)

The Roman Catholic Church along with many others teach a system of works to attain and keep salvation. These teachers are false prophets teaching another gospel for salvation and cannot therefore be saved themselves unless they abandon their false gospels and embrace the truth. The Rev. Billy Graham has paved the way for the Van Impe type mentality by compromising standards of separation from apostasy by yoking up with liberals, moderates, and unsaved clergy over the years in evangelism!

It certainly is much simpler to believe anything and accept everything and everybody's doctrines, but to do so is to say there are no absolutes in truth and that God is mutable. Popularity and profit no doubt have paved the way thus far for the preaching and teaching of the pre-trib rapture doctrine. Is it any wonder that the doctrine was absolutely unheard of until about 150 years ago?

Imagine 1800 years of church history passing before anyone was "spiritual" enough to "discover" the pre-trib rapture doctrine. The church has always held (church history will back this up) that Christians would be assaulted with afflictions, trials, persecutions, tribulations and every other type demonic attack, from the ascension of Jesus, culminating with the appearance and manifestation of the mystery of iniquity, the Antichrist, who would attack and martyr Christians nearly blotting out the mention of the name of Christ on earth! They held that after this attack and brief world rule by the Son of Perdition, that Jesus would come back, remove His people briefly, catching them away to the judgement seat of Christ, while bringing judgement on the forces of Antichrist. At the end of this judgement, they taught Jesus would return with His saints to subdue the world, destroy the Antichrist and his armies and bring in the millennium. This is what the mainstream Bible-believing church believed for almost one thousand eight hundred years. I need to state here plainly and emphatically that this book and the chart I have designed is an identical parallel with the traditional view on the second coming of Christ from church history. Truth must be recovered in order to unite a divided church on such an important subject.

When Antichrist comes to power and as the blood of saints flow in the streets under His sword, I wonder how many pre-tribist Christians will be driven to doubt God's word, love, and care, as well their salvation because they were not raptured before the appearance of the final man of sin. If this book is successful in turning the church back to the truth, those who have supported the pre-trib heresy the most, such as Dr. LaHaye and others like him, will suffer great financial loss and popularity. If they do come across to see this relevant truth they will need to exhaust their wealth in order to undo the damage their pre-trib literature has done to the church. Either way they will lose greatly.

"The Tribulation" of Matt. 24 is <u>Not</u> Daniel's Entire 70th Week, But Rather the Entire N.T. Church Age From the Destruction of Jerusalem Ending at the Cosmic Disturbances of Matt. 24:29 (which is the same event as is recorded in Revelation 6:12, The Sixth Seal) Outlined below.......

Our Savior plainly outlined the entire church age <u>in tribulation</u> until He comes...

1. False Christs would come in His name and deceive many. Matt. 24:5.

2. Wars and rumors of wars causing fear to many. Matt. 24:9.

3. Great and small nations would be at war with each other. Matt. 24:7.

4. Worldwide famines, plagues, pestilences, and earth quakes in many places. Matt. 24:7.

5. God's people could expect to be delivered up by godless rulers, kings and people, and be tormented physically and even killed. Matt. 24:9.

6. God's true people would be hated by <u>all</u> nations. Matt. 24:9.

7. Offense, hatred, and betrayal would abound. Matt. 24:10.

8. False prophets would arise and deceive many. Matt. 24:11.

9. Sin would become so prevalent that it would destroy the natural love of many, it would wax cold. Matt. 24:12.

10. The gospel (plan of salvation) would be preached in all of the world. (Anyone who would think the gospel of the kingdom does not include the saving gospel of Christ, which is the power of God until salvation, is certainly deceived).

11. Matthew 24 also contains a triple prophecy concerning first the destruction of Jerusalem in 70 A.D. by a prototype of Antichrist at the <u>beginning</u> of the N.T. church age, and then a final appearance of the real man of sin at the <u>end</u> of the church age, or the tribulation of "those days" - Vs. 15-21, and thirdly, a warning to the 144,000 sealed Jews of Revelation to flee Antichrist!

Now it is simple to realize that nearly 2,000 years, or 2 days have expired since our Lord ascended back to heaven. We who are living in these "last days" as spoken of by Paul surely are in the last moments of them just about to see the appearance of the Antichrist.

Who is foolish enough to say the last 2,000 years of church history has: 1) Not seen much fulfillment of our Lord's prophecy... 2) Been a golden messianic time of peace... 3) Not been great trouble, trial, and affliction on the people of God!

Christians wake up and realize we are living in the end of the 2,000 years of tribulation, i.e. "the tribulation of those days" which will culminate with the opening of the sixth seal, the cosmic disturbances, the rapture of the church and the beginning of the Day of the Lord! For 1800 years the church stood on this truth!

Chapter III

Tim LaHaye's Errors

Dr. Tim LaHaye has written, "No Fear of the Storm," one of the most representative books of our time on the pre-trib rapture doctrine. Of course, he totally endorses it. In reading it through, though not minutely, I felt that by answering the majority of his arguments for the doctrine, I could more easily expose the major fallacies and weaknesses in the pre-trib camp.

Error 1 - On page 15 and 14 at the bottom he quotes I Thess. 4:16-18 as a verse teaching the any moment (imminent) return of Christ. The answer here is a simple reading of this verse plainly shows it is merely teaching a "sure" return of Christ for our comfort (See vs. 18). He also quotes John 14:1-3 with the same import in mind. Thus, he plainly adds his doctrine of imminence to two scriptures where it does not exist. The real subtle move here by him is to try to equate an imminent return with a sure return by misapplying scripture. Read it for yourself!

Error 2 - On page 18 top he uses 1 John 3:3, identically as in error one, equating imminent return with sure return where imminent (any moment) does not exist.

Error 3 - On page 24 m., he states that the Christians of the first three centuries believed in an imminent (any moment) return of Christ. The simple fact is that the church for 1800 years only believed in an imminent post-trib rapture, only imminent, however, after certain prophecies were fulfilled. The horrible sufferings and persecutions God's people underwent for centuries under fore-runners of the Antichrist, many times convinced them that certainly Christ would come soon or at any moment for them. They plainly realized that the scriptures taught that the Antichrist must first come before Christ could come, II Thess. 2:1-3. The mainstream church switched to the imminent pre-trib rapture fantasy only after Darby began to widely teach it. The church has traditionally believed that the rapture could not take place until certain signs took place first such as the appearance of the Antichrist, restoration of Israel, etc.

Error 4 - On page 24, he claims that I Thess. 1:6-10 teaches an any moment return of Christ, but a simple reading shows plainly that we are to "...wait for His son from heaven...", i.e. wait patiently, not to expect Him any moment without a forewarning. Here is a flagrant disregard for literal interpretation of scripture. This is very serious indeed.

Error 5 - On page 32 b. and 33, he teaches that the rapture will happen in the twinkling of an eye and that all saved will suddenly vanish from earth and that the unsaved will not see it since it will happen so fast. The simple fact of scripture is that the rapture does not happen in the twinkling of an eye. The Bible says plainly that, WE WILL BE <u>CHANGED</u> IN THE TWINKLING OF AN EYE. Read I Cor. 15:51-54. Our bodies will be changed in the twinkling of an eye, and then we will be caught up to meet Christ in the air. Our ascension will no doubt be like our Savior's, very observable. See Acts 1:9. Another sad mishandling of scripture.

Error 6 - On page 34, he states that at the rapture babies will suddenly disappear. No doubt he is saying that all young and innocent babies and children who have not reached the age of accountability will be raptured. Plainly it needs to be stated for all that the rapture is only for those who are <u>in</u> Christ Jesus, and that by being <u>born-again</u> (See I Thess. 4:16) only those <u>In Christ</u> will be taken. To receive a glorified body these babies and small children would be bypassing salvation without first coming to the age of accountability, then being born-again to receive an eternal, incorruptible body. Here is an example of a bleeding heart seeking not to worry parents of babies and small children, and thus creating a doctrine of salvation for some without being born-again through repentance and faith in the Lord Jesus Christ. Very serious error.

Error 7 - On page 32 b. he says that the rapture will be instant, that no one will see it, then contradicts himself by using the catching up of Jesus and Elijah as examples showing the catching up as observable (see pg. 35 bottom and 36 top). Mr. LaHaye is confused on Bible facts. Mr. LaHaye, which is it? Snatched up in the twinkling of an eye or changed in the twinkling of an eye and <u>then</u> caught up as Jesus and Elijah were as an observable event as the scriptures teach? Thus pre-trib confusion mounts.

Error 8 - On page 40-41, Mr. LaHaye clearly defines the entire 70th week of Daniel as "the hour of wrath" to try the whole world. A major error. This is contrary to scripture which plainly places the wrath of God beginning <u>AFTER</u> the cosmic disturbances, announces the Day of the Lord (the sun darkened and moon turning to blood) at the opening of the sixth seal of Revelation (see Rev. 6:16-17 and Matt. 24:29). In calling all of the 70th week of Daniel the "hour of wrath," Mr. LaHaye erroneously insinuates that the men begging for the mountains to fall on them are in response to the first seals of Rev. 6. In reality, they are not motivated to flee in fear <u>until</u> the heavens depart as a scroll and they see the wrathful face of Him sitting on the throne only <u>after</u> the opening of the sixth seal. The rapture will take place before the wrathful Day of the Lord begins.

Error 9 - On page 46, Mr. LaHaye states the church age started in 33 A.D. and ends at the rapture. The fact is that the church includes saints of all ages, both Jews and Gentiles, bond and free, all are in Christ Jesus and will be raptured and caught up, or resurrected and caught up to meet Christ at His coming. Paul made this plain when he was writing the Thessalonians concerning those who sleep in Jesus will God bring with Him. To say Old Testament Jews were not members of the body of Christ is to repudiate their salvation. The Old Testament saints were saved by the same Jesus that the New Testament saints were, and are. The mystery hidden in the Old Testament and now revealed in the New was that the Gentiles would be members of the <u>same</u> body the common denominator being salvation through the blood of the cross for all (see Eph. 1:22-23 and all of chapter 3). Jesus shed his blood for all Old Testament saints!

A good pastor told us, in ignorance I am sure, that at the rapture only the New Testament saints were going to be raised and come back from heaven to reunite with their bodies. This would leave the Old Testament saints in the grave and their souls still in heaven at the time of the rapture. Absolutely zero scriptures teach this. Furthermore, if this were true, it would mean the Old Testament saints would be only spectators at the rapture and marriage supper of the Lamb. What an insult to priests, prophets, and holy men of old (much more godly than any today) if this were the case. No. Saints of all ages will be included at the rapture (I Thess. 4:13-14 and Eph. 1:10).

Error 11 - Mr. LaHaye says on pgs 45-46 that there is silence concerning the church in Revelation chapters 6-18 and that silence shows the church is gone. The simple answer is that the word "church" means "ekklesia" or "called out assembly." The called out assembly is seen as follows: In Chapter 6:9-10, the members of the church, His body, in heaven having been slain on earth by the Antichrist <u>during</u> the first seals. In Chapter 7:3-17, the servants of God were sealed in their foreheads. The servants of who? Satan or Christ? Of Christ. Thus if <u>of</u> Christ then they must be <u>in</u> Christ to be of Him. Else not of Him. If "in Christ," then members of His body, flesh of His flesh, bone of His bone. These 144,000 Jewish members of the church on earth were sealed <u>before</u> the opening of the seventh seal which ushers in the wrath of God to try the whole earth. Yes, 144,000 Jewish members of the body of Christ. The church. These Jews will still receive their Abrahamic promises of inheritance along with all true Jews of all ages. Remember, Jews and Gentiles who are saved are all members of "one body." Different members of the body of Christ will receive different inheritances in the millennium but will still be of <u>one</u>

body. These 144,000 Jews were left here to re-populate the earth during the millenium and are sealed to protect them from the great judgements of wrath beginning after the sixth seal. The rest of God's people were raptured at the appearance of Christ immediately after the sixth seal and before the wrath of God is poured out. Thus, members of the body of Christ, the church, are on earth in Revelation. Next Rev. ch. 8. The church is not seen here because this chapter, along with chapters 9-11, deals with describing the judgements of the wrath of God on earth. Chapter 12 gives a historical/prophetical parenthesis of Israel's travail and birth of Christ. She certainly is a member of His body. Verses 14-17 are clearly showing the members of the body of Christ on earth during the last 3-1/2 years along with the remnant of Israel's seed, probably new Jewish believers. These Jewish and possible Gentile believers (those Gentiles possibly saved during the last half of Daniel's 70th week) are members of the body of Christ and thus members of the church, the called out assembly. It must be noted that though the 144,000 were sealed from the plagues of the great day of God's wrathful judgements, they are still in physical fragile bodies subject to limitations, pain and death, identical to those Jews in Egypt who were kept from the death angel by the blood above and on the sides of the door posts. Thus Satan through the Antichrist is able to make war on them and it is these who the scriptures refer to as those who endure to the end, the same shall be saved. These are members of the body of Christ, the church, though they have certain earthly inheritances as Jews. Thus the church is seen in chapter 12. Chapters 13 and 14 again give us an historical prophetical view of Daniel's 70th week. The church is seen here as saints in Ch. 13, vs. 7, and the Antichrist making war on it (them) at the beginning of the 70th week (first 3-1/2 years). These are the same saints as seen in Rev. 6:9&7:14). All saints are members of the body of Christ the church. Chapter 15-18 pictures judgements of the coming last plagues of the last 3-1/2 years. Thus it is plain to see the church of God, the church of Christ (not denominational) or the body of Christ on earth during Daniel's 70th week.

Mr. LaHaye's, as well as all pre-tribists, erroneous doctrinal stand or statement of faith on Revelation Chapters 6-18 therefore must be as follows: There are no saints on earth during the 70th week of Daniel but these saints arc not in Christ because to be in Christ is to be of Christ and to be of Christ is to be of His body, and to be of His body is to be a member of His body, to be a member of His body is to be flesh of His flesh, and bone of His bone, and thus a member of the Church, which can't be. Also, they would belong to Christ's called out assembly or ekklesia, the church, and thus being a blood-washed believer would place the church in the 70th week of Daniel and this can't be. (Pretty sad isn't it!)

Error 12 - On page 47, he places the time of the wrath of God during Daniel's 70th week beginning in Rev. 6:1 - 18:24, but this is clearly incorrect. The time of wrath runs from 6:12 and on. The fact is that the ungodly do not sense, feel, nor see wrath until the cosmic disturbances in Rev. 6:12-18, when the sixth seal is opened and they <u>see</u> the heavens opened and an angry God seated on the throne. Here again, we have plain scriptural truth versus interpretation.

Error 13 - Page 47. If remnants of the church are not here during the 70th week of Daniel, then why would the gospel be entrusted to 144,000 non-Christians? Did not Jesus give the great commission to the church and the church alone? Pre-tribists teach that the 144,000 will be the evangelists during that time period. To say that they will preach only kingdom gospel only falls with the fact that kingdom gospel must include the saving gospel of Christ to win the lost.

Error 14 - He further makes the claim that the pre-trib position is a result of a much more literal understanding of scripture. This simply is not the case when one of their cornerstone arguments is examined, namely their wresting of II Thess. 2:7 into a dogma, and that through a radical interpretation. Most pre-tribists say this verse teaches a removal (?) of the Holy Spirit from the earth. The simple fact is as follows: 1) The word Holy Spirit is not used in this verse, 2) This verse does not say the Holy Spirit is removed from earth, 3) The restrainer in this verse is <u>not</u> named and therefore open to debate who or what it really is, 4) To say that the church here is removed with the Holy Spirit in this verse is 100% speculative. As crazy as it may seem, most pre-tribs are dogmatic on this interpretation even to the point of breaking, or withdrawing fellowship from anyone who differs from them.

Error 15 - Page 51. Mr. LaHaye states matter of factly that the seal judgements take 21 months, the trumpets 21 months, and the vials the last 42 months of the 70th week. I am sorry to inform him that there is <u>no proof</u> to this claim that can be offered. This is purely speculative and in fact plainly in error. We are giving proof in our book and chart that the Bible teaches the first six seals fill the first 3-1/2 years, the seventh seal, all the trumpets and vials the remaining 3-1/2 years (approximately). Here, Mr. LaHaye has forced his own interpretation, or rather fabrication, upon scripture. His 21 months have absolutely no scriptural credibility. If he wants to present this figure as a <u>guess</u> then I have no problem with that, even though he is wrong. This is a very serious departure from revealing truth.

Error 16 - On page 55 top, Mr. LaHaye quotes Rev. 7:14 regarding the martyred saints of the first part of the 70th week. He says plainly that they are not part of the church. Now dear friend I must ask you, since this verse plainly says these saints "have washed their robes and made them white in the blood of the Lamb...," doesn't it stand to reason that they are born-again believers? Now how in heaven's name can any man be a born-again believer without the Holy Spirit birthing them into God's family? If the Holy Spirit regenerated them then He also baptized them into the body of Christ. I Cor. 12:13 plainly says that all believers are baptized by the Spirit into the body of Christ. Ephesians tells us (1:22-23), "And hath put all things under his feet, and gave him to be the head over all things to the <u>church which is His body</u>, the fullness of Him that filleth all in all." Naturally, they cannot be a part of the church, according to Mr. LaHaye and other pre-tribs, because these are found martyred out of the first 3-1/2 years of Daniel's 70th week and the church has already supposedly been removed along with the Holy Spirit. Again, the word of God is sadly violated. Mr. LaHaye needs to heed the golden rule of interpretation found on page 240 of his book..."When the plain sense of Scripture makes common sense, seek no other sense, but take every word at its primary, literal meaning unless the facts of the immediate context clearly indicate otherwise."

Error 17 - On page 61. I Thess. 4:13-18 is totally misrepresented. These verses were not written to give comfort to saints concerning escape from the coming tribulation or any part of it. Verse 13 shows plainly Paul was <u>comforting</u> the saints concerning them which "sleep in Christ." The comfort of verse 13 and 18 is that those in Christ who departed by death will be brought back to meet their loved ones at the rapture. Here again, Mr. LaHaye departs from his golden rule of interpretation.

Error 18 - He teaches of page 62 that special grace will be given to those who are saved after the rapture, since this period is the wrath of God. The truth in reality is, if it would be unjust to allow the church to enter the 70th week of Daniel, then it would be equally unjust to allow some one to stay in that time period without instantly rapturing them also. (I can just imagine now after exposing this heresy that the pre-tribs will be ready to invent a doctrine that says any one being saved in Daniel's 70th week will be instantly raptured. Mr. LaHaye has already endorsed the innocent baby/child rapture so why not this?

Further, it needs to be added that the first 3-1/2 years of the 70th week of Daniel is plainly the wrath of Satan on believers while the Antichrist also sets up a temporary kingdom of peace, while the last 3-1/2 years falls under the wrath of God on the inhabitants of the earth after the rapture. Nowhere in scripture are we given comfort that God will keep us out of tribulations, persecutions, or afflictions, nor even death at the hands of Satan or his emissaries. Keeping us through, yes. Out of, no. A simple reading of Foxes Book of Martyrs will show this. (Pre-trib doctrine teaches that we are exempt from those things and it is interesting to note that the pre-trib doctrine is the most widespread in cultures that are very prosperous and where Christians have the most wealth and freedoms with the least persecutions. This is the case with America. The electronic church with its "prosperity gospel," the Copeland ministries and others like it, are great strong holds for the pre-trib rapture heresy. In 1996, Christians who are suffering for their faith financially or physically are held up in scorn by these type ministries, and even by the fundamental church, as people who must not somehow be right with God suffering so, and probably don't have the right kind of faith to deliver themselves.

Error 19 - On page 63, he claims that if Christ does not rapture the church before the 70th week begins, then the "blessed hope" becomes the "blasted hope." The fact is that Paul's blessed hope in Titus 2:13 is not a blasted hope simply because the church will go through severe persecution and trial. The comfort of the rapture is <u>not</u> comfort that we will be spared any part or all of the 70th week but rather that 1) Though Christ departed He is coming back for us with our departed loved ones in Christ, 2) To deliver us to himself out of this sinful world, 3) To a place He has prepared for us, 4) Which is far better to depart and be with Christ.

Here again, a serious misapplication of scripture. If some think that I am unfairly targeting Mr. LaHaye - remember this - Mr. LaHaye placed <u>himself</u> in the position as a lightening rod for the pre-trib rapture doctrine by widely writing and preaching on it. Therefore when the lightening of God's rebuke at his doctrine falls at his feet no one should be surprised. The lightening of God's rebuke in this case is in this paper simply as an expose of his flagrant disregard for rightly dividing and applying the simple truths of God's word. Mr. LaHaye is merely parroting traditional pre-trib doctrine; and plainly shows he is not a theologian in any sense, though he may be very sincere. I am sure he is a devout follower of Christ but he needs to take his seat on the back or rather front pew and relearn the principles of sound Biblical/doctrinal exegesis. The scriptures plainly teach afflictions, trial, and persecutions would be the lot of those who remain faithful to Christ. "Yea all that live godly in Christ Jesus shall suffer persecution."

Error 20 - Mr. LaHaye says that the coming of Christ was imminent in the first century church. The fact is it has never been imminent until certain scriptures were fulfilled; such as the revealing of the Antichrist. II Thess. 2:1-3 plainly tells us that the coming of Christ and our gathering together unto Him could not take place until first there would be an apostasy and that the man of sin be revealed. This is literally to be believed and not to be interpreted. By the way, revealed to who? The unsaved? Or the church? Only a revealing of the Antichrist to the church could fulfill this prophecy.

Error 21 - He quotes I John 3:3 to try to prove an imminent return is the greatest incentive to holy living. This verse on the other hand is not teaching an imminent return of Christ as an incentive for holy living, but rather that the hope of His coming again in itself is an incentive for holy living. Mr. LaHaye does not see this.

Error 22 - Further on page 65, he says that not believing in imminence takes off our guard in a spiritual sense to holy living. I ask you what about the following incentives to holy living: 1) Loss of the joy of salvation, 2) Loss of rewards, 3) Fear of stumbling a weaker brother or sister and setting a poor example as a Christian, 4) Chastisement for sin in our lives, 5) Displeasing our Savior, 6) Loss of position in the church, 7) Tarnishing our testimony and causing the unsaved to reject our testimony, etc.

If the pre-tribs only incentive for holy living is that Christ could come at any moment, then the idea comes across that they don't want to get caught in sin as a primary motive for holy living. I am a strong personal soul winner, and nothing bothers me more than the prospect that if I don't live a godly Christian life, people will not see Christ in me and will not accept my testimony when I witness to them.

Error 23 - On page 65 bottom, he claims that Jesus and the apostles taught imminence, or an any moment return of Christ. Certain things must first be fulfilled. A sure coming, yes. An any moment coming, no. (Did our Savior tell His disciples in Matt. 24 that after His ascension he could come back at any moment? See His discourse just before this section.)

Error 24 - On page 66, he claims for one not to believe in the imminent, any moment return of Christ, means you cannot even look for His return. If this is true then the same could be said about His first coming. Then the wise men could not have looked forward to His first coming because it was not imminent. They were plainly looking for the sign of his first coming, the star of David. We are to watch for certain signs such as the regathering of the Jews to their homeland, the budding of the fig tree, as well as the revealing of the Antichrist. Did this fact keep the world of saints from looking forward to His first coming? Absolutely not! So neither should it affect our attitudes of great eagerness to see Christ come again though certain things must first be fulfilled.

Error 25 - On page 66, he claims that those who reject the pre-trib position are <u>looking for</u> (subtly insinuating <u>forward to</u>) the coming of Antichrist. This is offensively slanderous to our true doctrinal position and he knows it. So anxious is he to build his straw house haven of safety from the coming Antichrist, that he becomes totally insensitive to the pure and godly motives of those who disagree with him.

Error 26 - On page 74 bottom and 76 top, he claims Rev. 4:1-2 refers to the rapture. Here again, an <u>interpretation</u> of literal scriptural truth rather than taking it at face value. These verses simply do not refer to the rapture. They simply state John receiving a heavenly view of prophetic vision. Similarity is not identity. Who says John is representative of the church here? Again, a forced interpretation. This is the reason we have so many cults today, because they interpret scripture to mean other than what it really says, or because Dr. so and so said so.

Error 27 - On page 101, he claims that anything other than a pre-trib rapture would not be a blessed hope. The fact is that the blessed hope does not refer to the Christian escaping the terrors of the Antichrist, but rather for Christians to rejoice with great joy that Jesus <u>is</u> coming back one day. We will not be left here unattended by our shepherd. Many Christians have sealed their faith with blood. Did they miss the blessed hope? I think not.

Error 28 - That the seals of Rev. 6 are terrible times on earth there is no doubt but they are not the wrath of God. God deals today on earth, AIDS, famine, tornadoes, etc. All exist no doubt from His hand or the permissive will of God. Shall we not receive evil at the hand of God as well as good? Job thought so. See Job 2:10. Remember two types of evil exist, moral evil and physical evil. We will never receive moral evil from God for God can not sin nor tempteth he any man to sin. James 1:13.

Error 29 - Here again on page 107 he pushes the imminent, any moment, return of our Lord without any regard to the fact that that day could not come until the apostasy takes place first and that man of sin be revealed. In II Thess. 2:1-3 the pre-tribs generally (and erroneously) divorce the term "Day of Christ" from the "gathering together unto Him (rapture)." They must do this or else that would mean that the Antichrist must appear first before the rapture could take place as the scriptures plainly teach. This is plainly a wresting of scripture. The pre-tribs wrest this verse out of its context and relegate it to the end of the 70th week of Daniel rather than leave it where it belongs, referring to the return of Christ as the rapture, in 1:10 and 2:1. As a pre-trib for twenty-five years I was taught the Day of the Lord and the Day of Christ were two different events. They are not.

Error 30 - The restrainer of II Thess. 2:7 is probably not the Holy Spirit since the restrainer is taken out of, or steps aside from, the way to the revealing of the Antichrist. This would be theologically impossible especially if He were to be taken out of the world and the church with Him. (As most pre-tribs teach) The world is not in cooperation with the Holy Spirit; so the Holy Spirit cannot do less than a perfect job to restrain sin. To do less, i.e. to allow the Antichrist to appear, would be for Him to author sin. The word of God does not say "Holy Spirit," pre-tribs say it, then proceed to remove the Holy Spirit from the earth with the church and establish this false interpretation as a dogma. The restrainer is probably the restraint built into our systems of law and order, which are based upon Roman law dating back to the time of Christ; and then personified by being judicially executed and applied by those in government until they are set aside or overthrown by abounding lawlessness. Thus, the two essential elements, personal and impersonal, as indicated by II Thess. 2:7.

C.G. Findlay, as a Greek scholar, in his book "The Epistles of Paul the Apostle to the Thessalonians" says on page 178-179:

> "St. Paul's political acumen, guided by his prophetical inspiration, was competent to distinguish between the character and personal action of the Emperor-god and the grand fabric of the Roman Empire over which he presided. As head of the civil state, the reigning Augustus was the impersonation of law, while in his character as a man, and in his assumption of deity, he might be the type of the most profane and wanton lawlessness (witness Caligula, Nero, Elagabalus.) Roman law and the authority of the magistrate formed a breakwater against the excesses of autocratic tyranny as well as of popular violence. The absolutism of the bad Caesars had after all its limit; their despotic power trampled on the laws and was yet restrained by them...Nero fell; and the Roman State remained, to be the restrainer of lawlessness and, so far, a protector of infant Christianity. Wiser rulers and better times were in store for the Empire. Through the ages the katexov of the Apostolic times has proved a bulwark of society. In the crisis of the 8th century

"the laws of Rome saved Christianity from Saracen dominion more than the armies... The torrent of Mohammedan invasion was arrested for 700 years." As long as Roman law was cultivated in the Empire and administered under proper control, the invaders of Byzantine territory were everywhere unsuccessful" (Finlay, History of Byzantine Empire, pp. 27f.) Nor did Roman law fall with the Empire itself, any more than it rose therefrom. It allied itself with systems of Christendom. Meanwhile, Caesarism also survive a second legacy from Rome and a word of evil omen, the title and model of illegal sovereignty. The lawlessness of human nature holds this "mystery" in solution, ready to precipitate itself and "to be revealed at the last season." The mystery betrays its working in partial and transitional manifestations, until "in its season" it crystallizes into its complete expression. Let reverence for law disappear in public life along with religious faith, and there is nothing to prevent a new Caesar becoming master and god of the civilized world armed with immensely greater power...

Lawlessness then escalates to a point to produce "ek mesou gentai" (Greek for "Out of the midst comes to be"). Simply spoken, the Antichrist will arise out of the midst of lawlessness when the system and agent of restraint have reached the completion of their restraint. Not the Holy Spirit and the church.

Error 31 - On page 111, Mr. LaHaye states matter of factly that the rapture does not appear in the Olivet discourse. The fact is that the rapture does indeed appear there if you can believe Jesus in Matt. 24:31 where He comes and gathers His elect from the four winds. This event takes place immediately after the cosmic disturbances (sun darkening and moon turning to blood) and is identical in time sequence therefore to Rev. 6:12 at the sixth seal opening and the identical same cosmic disturbances. This is plainly the beginning of the day of the Lord, and we who are saved are promised to be raptured immediately before it begins. Here again the pre-tribs are guilty of wresting scripture and forcing an interpretation instead of taking the Bible literally at face value. Note as follows: (Irrefutable) The scripture, Matt. 24:29, does not say "Immediately after Daniel's 70th week (or even after the seven years of tribulation). It says "Immediately after the tribulation OF THOSE DAYS." What days? Mark uses the term "affliction" of those days. What days? Simple, the days of waiting for the return of Jesus from the destruction of Jerusalem through all the afflictions and tribulations the church would go through up until the appearance and final persecution of Antichrist.

<u>Day</u> equals <u>one</u>, <u>days</u> equal <u>two</u>. Easily 2,000 years of church history (2 days) before the Son of God would return. The affliction of 2,000 years of church history culminating with the Antichrist and the six seals, would produce the coming of Christ and the beginning of the Day of the Lord. Remember, the disciple asked Him <u>When</u> would these things be, and <u>What</u> would be the sign of His coming and the sign of the end of the world. (Notice they asked what <u>sign</u> would specifically predate his appearing. He said nothing about a secret coming in a secret rapture). Our Lord plainly answered them by giving them a complete view of 2,000 years of church history ending at his coming. What He was simply and plainly saying was, "Immediately after the afflictions and tribulation of the ages of church history (from the destruction of Jerusalem until the final persecution of the coming Antichrist) the sun will darken and moon turn to blood which is exactly what happens at the sixth seal.

Again, I want to emphasize, the scripture does not say, "Immediately after Daniel's 70th week," as both pre- and modern post Daniel's seventh week claim. This cannot be refuted. Scripture means what it says and says what it means. The pre-tribs as well as the modern post-tribs say Matt. 24:29-31 is at the end of the 70th week of Daniel. The pre-tribs say the gathering of the elect is a Jewish gathering of their elect to inherit the millennial earth, while the modern post tribs say this is the rapture after the 70th week of Daniel. Both are wrong. The truth is that the gathering of the elect is immediately after the 2,000 or so years of church history, i.e. the rapture and the gathering of all saved.

The Bible says, "From the uttermost part of heaven (souls in heaven) unto the uttermost part of the earth or all those saved waiting to be raptured at His second coming." Matt. 24:40-41 makes this very clear. "Then shall two be in the field, the one shall be taken, and the other left. Two women shall be grinding at the mill; the one shall be taken and the other left..." It needs to be noted that when this takes place it will be sudden and unexpected to the wicked as it was in the days of Noah (vs. 38 & 39). These were not the wicked being taken to judgement as the pre-tribs teach, but rather the saints at the rapture confirmed by vs. 42.

Chapter IV

Summing Up Holes in the Pre-Trib Rapture Position
That Are Too Vast
To Close Without Wresting Scripture

1. No scripture says the Holy Spirit will be removed from the earth and the church with Him. That idea is a forced interpretation of II Thess. 2:7 and has no doctrinal support at all.

2. No scripture teaches the church or a remnant of it will not be here and thus escape the first 3-1/2 years of Daniel's 70th week.

3. Jesus plainly told the disciples that they would suffer persecution and imprisonment and yea, even death for their faith until He comes. This warning did not destroy their love and looking for their Savior nor should it us.

4. The Day of the Lord begins the wrath of God announced by cosmic disturbances at the sixth seal which identically parallels Matt. 24:29-31, not at the end of Daniel's 70th week.

5. For almost 1800 years of church history, the pre-trib imminent rapture doctrine did not exist.

6. The pre-trib rapture position can only be arrived at by wresting, mis-applying, and interpreting scripture to mean what it does not.

7. "Immediately after the tribulation of those days" has a forced interpretation by both pre- and modern post-tribs as "Immediately after Daniel's 70th week."

8. II Thess. 2:7 and Matt. 24:29 have been added to (though probably through ignorance) by pre-tribs thus, 1) Corrupting the word of God on this subject, 2) Forcing the scriptures to say what it does not, and 3) Spread heresy and false doctrine lulling the church to sleep. This position must be abandoned.

9. The Day of the Lord as spoken of in Joel and other Old Testament passages, is plainly to be immediately preceded by two cosmic distur-bances, the sun darkening and the moon turning to blood. Then proceeds

not the millennium (as Dr. LaHaye and other pre-tribs say, see his chart on page 72 of his book) but rather an unparalleled time of God's wrath being poured out on earth identically coinciding the event with the opening of the sixth seal in Revelation 6. This cannot be refuted.

10. If the rapture is to be pre-trib imminent, sudden and secret and the ungodly of Rev. 6 are six seals into the 70th week of Daniel, then why is it that they didn't realize Christ had already come some three years earlier and had already caught out the church? The rapture in that case would have certainly split and devastated families by the hundreds of thousands giving those knowledgeable in prophecy who were not saved the clear truth that Christ had returned and they were left. This would clearly be announced to the entire world forcing them to admit to the truth of what had happened. This would then cause the unsaved to realize their impending doom immediately after the supposed pre-trib rapture, and especially after the seals as they begin to be opened. No! The wicked will be plainly caught unawares. Not so, though if a rapture had happened 3-1/2 years or so earlier. The unsaved will be saying peace and safety and lulling in the false security of rule under the man of sin. I Thess. 1:2-4 vividly shows this. "For yourselves know perfectly that the day of the Lord so cometh as a thief in the night. For when they shall say peace and safety; then sudden destruction cometh upon them as travail upon a woman with child; and they shall not escape."

More Serious Problems of the Pre-trib Imminent Rapture Heresy

1. It promotes a system of forced, false theological beliefs and interpretations and is then proclaimed as unshakable dogma. Any time an English translation of the Greek speaks somewhat obscurely, the reader must not be dogmatic and read into that obscurity that which it does not say. II Thess. 2:7 is a perfect example. Pre-tribists dogmatically, with an infallible attitude, say this is the Holy Spirit. So also with Matt. 24:31 making "of those days" to read "Daniel's 70th week."

2. The pre-trib rapture doctrine has lulled the church to sleep. In 1996, soul winning, consecration, separation, etc. is at an all time low. The church has come to relax her vigilance against forces of Antichrist believing she will not have to face persecution yea even death, but will be delivered from Antichrist. Unless she wakes up to the truth, no doubt she will be caught completely off guard. In 1942, the ships in Pearl Harbor had relaxed their vigilance against the Japanese and were catastrophically destroyed unmercifully. Thus, it will be when the Antichrist comes to

power. "He shall make war against the saints and shall overcome them. Revelation 13:7 and Daniel 7:21.

3. If a pre-trib rapture has just taken place and all saved people are gone then who will Antichrist have to make war with? How about that Doctor Even if there were a great revival with floods of people saved immediatel after a supposed pre-trib rapture, they would be only babes in Christ, (A revival under reign of Antichrist? Preposterous!). Besides who will be around to win them if the church is gone? Another point, some pre-tribist say that those who knew the truth but were not saved before the rapture will be saved after the rapture and become tribulation preachers. This is however, plainly contrary to scripture because "...they received not the love of the truth and therefore God shall send them a strong delusion tha they all might be damned who had pleasure in unrighteousness..." (I Thess. 2:10-13). The fact arises that the time immediately preceding the rapture is a hot bed of apostasy with little faith on the earth. (See Luke 18:8). When Jesus comes at the sixth seal He finds few saved on earth simply because most Christians were martyred under the Antichrist.

4. Concerning the 144,000 who some pre-tribs say will be the evangelist during the 70th week of Daniel after the church is pre-tribulationally raptured: Who wins them to Christ? How shall they hear without a preacher (Romans 10)? Who will have discipled them to be disciples if al Christians were raptured before the week begins? Did not Jesus command His disciples to disciple others?

5. If it is unjust for the church to enter the 70th week of Daniel, then i would be unjust for any souls to be saved and left behind (saved after the rapture) during the first 3-1/2 years since pre-tribs state that is a time of the wrath of God on earth. This would charge God with being unjust in allowing any of His sheep to stay on earth after Daniel's 70th week begins In that case, they would have to be instantly raptured the second they became born again. Shall we create a new doctrine here to accommodate pre-tribists?

6. Pre-tribists say the seal judgements are wrathful judgements of God on earth and thus, the church must be exempted by a pre-trib rapture. In reality, Revelation plainly shows the book with seals was opened seal by seal for John to "see" panoramic scenes to be unfolded before him. This was nearly 2,000 years ago when this happened as each seal was opened the panoramic scenes unfolded so John could record them. The sealed book and the loosing of the seals did not cause the judgements to take

place but rather previewed their occurrences. What God superintended and/or allows prophetically to occur and then records for His people, does not mean He has caused every event to take place. Besides this, the fact remains that similar four horsemen of the apocalypse have in many areas of the world, over the past two thousand years, galloped across nations, cities, and continents causing dictatorships, world wars, famines, rapid desecration of God's people and death. The main difference here though will be the four horsemen of the apocalypse will be given reign to gallop across the face of the entire earth during the 70th week of Daniel. I have no doubt that where these tragic calamities have happened and are even today taking place, those in such conditions feel as if they are in a veritable type of the first 1/2 of Daniel's 70th week.

I must quote Dr. Ironside, whom Dr. LaHaye quoted, "Be careful of any teaching that is new, it might not be true." While Mr. LaHaye used this in reference to the Mid-trib rapture position, I use it in regards to the pre-trib rapture position of Mr. LaHaye's. One hundred sixty-six (166) years old is new when compared to 1800 years of church history. This book and chart are nearly an identical, if not identical; parallel to the historic 1800 year doctrinal position of the church. Dave McPherson makes a valuable point on imminence in his book, "Rapture" (A very good book though we differ on the timing of the post-trib rapture). He points out the early church believed in "post-trib imminence" up until the 1800s when the pre-trib imminence doctrine was forged.

For 1800 years, the church believed the Lord could come at any moment due to the many trials they were going through and the types of Antichrist persecutions they were facing. These serious afflictions convinced them that the age in which they were living was therefore qualified for an imminent return of Christ. Imminent yes, but only as a post-trib imminence. "Yea even at the doors." Even so, come Lord Jesus. Thank you Mr. McPherson.

One last note needs to be made as to proof that the sixth seal is located in the middle of the week of Daniel. The Antichrist breaks his covenant in the middle of the week with Israel (Daniel 9). At this point, they are chased into the wilderness for <u>1,260 days or 3-1/2 years</u> (Rev. 12:6). The wrath of God begins at the sixth seal from which the 144,000 are sealed and thus protected from God's wrath as they flee. The Antichrist is empowered by Satan who is cast to earth (Rev. 12:7-13) in the middle of the week thus, corresponding to the exact time he sits in the temple showing himself to be God, thus betraying the Jews. Simply spoken, it is immediately after the sixth seal that the 144,000 are sealed. For how long? <u>1,260 days or 3-1/2 years</u> (Rev. 12:6). Thus the sixth seal immediately preceding the sealing of the 144,000 takes place in the middle of the week along with the rapture of the church since the cosmic disturbances of Matt. 24 (Rev. 6) take place immediately before the gathering of His elect (rapture).

Chapter V

The Threefold Application of Matt. 24:15-28
To Three Separate Generational Spheres
Of Gentile and Jewish Christians

Since Matt. 24:15-28 is <u>not a prophecy to be applied to only one particular Christian period of church history</u>, it can only be fully appreciated and understood by those Christians living in the actual scene of God's prophetic calendar in church history. There are three separate and distinct periods of church history that Matt. 24:15-28 applies to. Note carefully: three levels of overlapping prophecy ingrained in Matt. 24 (they are <u>not</u> interchangeable!)

1. Warnings to Christians <u>at the Olivet discourse</u> concerning the prophetical Destruction of Jerusalem, commanding them to flee.

2. Warnings to Christians <u>of all ages</u> concerning the long church age to come wracked by affliction and persecution culminating in the coming of the man of sin at the end of the church age, they also being commanded to flee him.

3. Warning to the <u>144,000 male Jewish virgins</u> (yes, who will also have the same Bible we have and read it) who will be here, not raptured after the sixth seal, to flee the Antichrist when he stands in the temple proclaiming himself to be God in the midst of the 70th week. These 144,000 are sealed from the seven trumpets and vials of the wrath of God, but must flee to the wilderness for 3-1/2 years since still physically vulnerable to Antichrist as Revelation teaches.

This third prophetic warning of Jesus to the 144,000 is <u>erroneously applied to the second group of Christians</u> living at the end of the tribulational and afflicted 2,000 years of the church age awaiting the rapture before the sixth seal. This is the reason the modern post-trib camp (not the post-trib position of <u>this</u> book) of the three camps has erroneously seen the church <u>fleeing</u> and not being raptured in the midst of Daniel's 70th week.

Undoubtedly, these 144,000 left behind in physical bodies will become those who re-populate the earth and re-build the twelve tribes during the millennium. Being on the run from the Antichrist, it is doubtful that they will be the evangelists during the last 3-1/2 years of Daniel's 70th week.

Remember, the people of earth were said to "not repent" because of their wickedness during the outpouring of God's wrath after the opening of the sixth seal. (Rev. 9:21).

Finally, the term "For then shall there be great tribulation such as was not since the beginning of the world..." Matt. 24:21 has <u>three</u> levels of application depending upon the group of believers and the point of time in which they live.

<u>Group One</u>: "Great tribulation" to the Jewish Christians of A.D. 66-70 referring to the coming desolation under the assault by Titus in 70 A.D.

<u>Group Two</u>: "Great tribulation" to the Christians alive at the end of the church age under certain attacks by the Antichrist during the first 3-1/2 years of Daniel's 70th week.

<u>Group Three</u>: "Great tribulation" to the 144,000 sealed Jews after the rapture referring to the attack of Antichrist during the last 3-1/2 years of Daniel's 70th week, when he as the abomination or desolation sits down in the temple of God showing himself to be God!

3 LEVELS OF PROPHECIES INGRAINED IN
MATT. 24:15-28

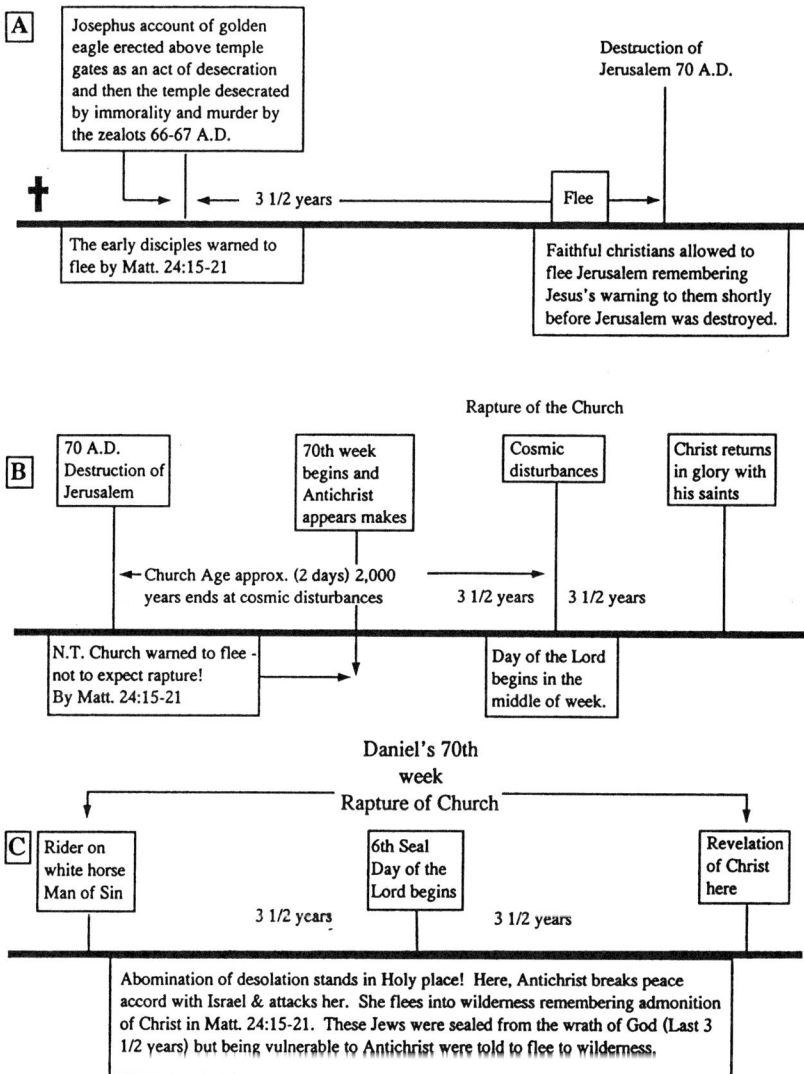

A | Josephus account of golden eagle erected above temple gates as an act of desecration and then the temple desecrated by immorality and murder by the zealots 66-67 A.D.

Destruction of Jerusalem 70 A.D.

✝   ← 3 1/2 years → | Flee

The early disciples warned to flee by Matt. 24:15-21

Faithful christians allowed to flee Jerusalem remembering Jesus's warning to them shortly before Jerusalem was destroyed.

Rapture of the Church

B | 70 A.D. Destruction of Jerusalem

70th week begins and Antichrist appears makes

Cosmic disturbances

Christ returns in glory with his saints

← Church Age approx. (2 days) 2,000 years ends at cosmic disturbances   3 1/2 years   3 1/2 years

N.T. Church warned to flee - not to expect rapture! By Matt. 24:15-21

Day of the Lord begins in the middle of week.

Daniel's 70th week

Rapture of Church

C | Rider on white horse Man of Sin

6th Seal Day of the Lord begins

Revelation of Christ here

3 1/2 years   3 1/2 years

Abomination of desolation stands in Holy place! Here, Antichrist breaks peace accord with Israel & attacks her. She flees into wilderness remembering admonition of Christ in Matt. 24:15-21. These Jews were sealed from the wrath of God (Last 3 1/2 years) but being vulnerable to Antichrist were told to flee to wilderness.

Matthew 24:21

*"For then shall there be great tribulation, such as was not since the beginning of the world t●
this time, nor ever shall be..."*

Our Lord was giving a threefold prophecy, vs. 13-22, concerning th●
destruction of Jerusalem first, then the coming and deification of the littl●
horn of Daniel in the end of the last days, and thirdly, a warning to th●
144,000 sealed Jews to flee the Antichrist in the midst of the week just afte●
he sits down in the temple proclaiming himself as God! (These 144,000 Jew●
were sealed but <u>not</u> raptured!) When Antichrist is <u>first</u> revealed he marche●
with military might and power against three of the ten nations of the revive●
Roman Empire (three of the little horns of Daniel) and destroys them. Th●
idea of a bow and no arrows does not especially show a bloodless victory sinc●
a bow and no arrows is utterly useless. A thief with a gun is not described a●
a thief with a gun <u>and bullets</u> since the bullets are taken for granted. No doub●
he institutes a virtual blood bath against the three nations and literall●
decimates them. He roots them up (Daniel 7:8), which can hardly be said o●
bloodless victory.

At the same time, he makes war on the saints of God, the church, an●
overcomes them. (I have no doubt that the pre-trib imminent rapture heres●
is responsible for the church being caught completely off guard, lulling then●
to sleep expecting to escape such a violent persecution from the man of sin●
Will not the blood of innocent Christians at least partially be charged to thos●
pre-trib proponents who falsely, though perhaps ignorantly, create a doctrina●
false haven of safety?) This military exercise of power and attack (1st seal) i●
clearly followed by the normal ravages of war; the chaos and bloodshed of th●
2nd seal with lawlessness in the streets; the famine under the 3rd seal; an●
finally on the heels of famine, plagues under the 4th seal. And remember, al●
natural consequences of war and unparalleled lawlessness on earth.

(After his conquering the entire earth, the Antichrist then in the middle o●
the week breaks his peace accord with Israel. See Daniel 9:26-27 and II Thess●
2:3-4. He then, true to form, makes war with the believing remnant of Israe●
and chases them into the wilderness. (See Rev. 12:12-17) This eventuall●
culminates in the battle of Armageddon.

A reading of Josephus' historical account of the destruction of Jerusalem●
and surrounding countries by Titus and his powerful armies, clearly shows th●
horrors were so great that never in the history of the world had there been●
such devastation and terror. According to historical accounts the Roman●
armies, after surrounding Jerusalem, withdrew for several days (unwittingly●
giving God's people time to flee the city across the Jordan into the mountain●

of Pella. No doubt the recent erecting of the golden eagle by the Romans above the temple gates (an abominable sign of the desecration of the temple by the Jews which the Jews promptly tore down), was fresh in the disciple's minds along with Christ's warning to flee found in these verses 13-22, when Titus arrived. The horror that will unfold under the last coming Antichrist, the superman of all previous Antichrists, will be a final fulfillment of these verses with a fair warning to God's people everywhere.

This great tribulation or affliction was plainly the great trouble that would come with Titus, another prototype of the man of sin, at the destruction of Jerusalem in 70 A.D. and then the true Antichrist in Revelation 6. God's people were warned to flee when they saw certain signs. Simply speaking up until the destruction of Jerusalem there had never before in the history of the world been such a devastation before a forerunner of the Antichrist, and then in the end of the world would come one last time of trouble (even surpassing Titus) under the final man of sin. Under the final Antichrist would come Armageddon, and the beginning of the judgements of the day of the Lord, along with the return of Christ. The pre-tribists, by equating the great tribulation the first 3-1/2 years with the wrath of God supposedly to begin with the first seal, forces the interpretation of a pre-70th week rapture. Now, why would our Savior warn his disciples to flee the coming Antichrist if they were going to be removed before the Antichrist's appearance? He simply and plainly warned them to flee or face certain death, and this warning is to us as well.

It may be well here to address the attempted application of Luke 21:36 to a supposed pre-trib rapture.

> "Watch ye therefore, and pray always, that ye may be accounted worthy to escape all these things that shall come to pass, and to stand before the Son of man."

This verse refers to a warning to be worthy. (Worthy refers to walk, not to salvation). To be counted worthy is indicative of a believer who's walk with Christ is consistently righteous and therefore he will: a) Escape Titus by obedience to Christ by fleeing Jerusalem, b) Escape Antichrist's persecution by fleeing when he is revealed (instead of looking for a false pre-trib rapture), c) As one of the 111,000, flee to the wilderness escaping the Antichrist when he violates his seven year peace accord with Israel in the midst of Daniel's 70th week. Being counted worthy to escape what things? Simply the great trouble of the first 3-1/2 years. By rapture? No, by obedient fleeing. Sorry, no rapture here.

Chapter VI

Critical Comments on I and II Thessalonians
Clearly Establishing The Rapture Taking Place At The Beginning and/or
Immediately Prior To The Day Of The Lord
Just After The Opening Of The Sixth Seal Signed By The
Same Cosmic Disturbances of Matt. 24:29, Joel 2:31 and Acts 2:20.

Clearly Paul felt it imperative to establish the Thessalonians in the following truth:

1. They were warned to expect persecutions, sufferings, and tribulation for their faith in Christ Jesus at the hands of the ungodly- I Thess. 2:15, 3:3-4

    "Who both killed the Lord Jesus, and their own prophets, and have persecuted us; and they please not God, and are contrary to all men...That no man should be moved by these afflictions; for yourselves know that we are appointed thereunto. For verily, when we were with you, we told you before that we should suffer tribulation; even as it came to pass, and ye know."

2. This warning was needed so they would not be tempted to give up their stand for Christ and were also told plainly that the wrath of God was appointed to those who rejected Christ and persecuted them-I Thess. 2:16

    "Forbidding us to speak to the Gentiles that they might be saved, to fill up their sins always for the <u>wrath</u> is come upon them to the uttermost." [Notice also II Thess. 1:6-10] "Seeing it is a righteous thing with God to recompense tribulation to them that trouble you; and to you who are troubled rest with us, when the Lord Jesus shall be revealed from heaven with His mighty angels, in flaming fire <u>taking vengeance on them</u> that know not God, and that obey not the gospel of our Lord Jesus Christ; who shall be punished with everlasting destruction from the presence of the Lord, and from the glory of His power; when He shall come to be <u>glorified in His saints,</u> and to be admired in all them that believe..."

It needs to be reminded that <u>this wrath</u> is not being placed in hell or the lake of fire, but rather the wrath of God being poured out during the first part of the day of the Lord, which begins with the cosmic disturbances, the trumpet, and vial judgements which immediately follow the return of Christ.

3. The encouragement of this warning was found in the glorious truth that Christ was coming back for them "with" all His saints - I Thess. 3:13.

> "To the end he may establish your hearts unblameable in holiness before God, even our Father, at the coming of our Lord Jesus Christ with all His saints."

It needs to be pointed out that all here does not point to His coming at the end of Daniel's 70th week due to the following: a) The context is indicative of the Thessalonians' needing to be aware of the blessed hope and appearing of Christ to bring punishment on those who were persecuting them which is just what happened at the sixth seal beginning the day of the Lord, b) When Jesus returns with all of His saints, He simply means that all of those saints, who from Adam until the rapture departed this life via death, will be brought back to earth from heaven, all including Old Testament saints. At the time of the rapture, I have no doubt that 95% (my speculation is as good as any) of the saints will come with Christ while only about 5% or less of the total will be here for the physical rapture without seeing death, c) Also, this verse is further enlarged on in the next chapter, the rapture chapter.

4. The need to further enlarge on I Thess. 3:13 (note no chapter-verse divisions in the original languages) is seen in the next chapter 4:15-18, as a means of comforting them.

> "For this we say unto you by the word of the Lord, that we which are alive and remain unto the coming of the Lord shall not prevent them which are asleep. For the Lord himself shall descend from heaven with a shout, with the voice of the archangel, and with the trump of God, and the dead in Christ shall rise first; then we which are alive and remain shall be caught up together with them in the clouds, to meet the Lord in the air; and so shall we ever be with the Lord. Wherefore comfort one another with these words."

5. The coming of Christ and our rapture to meet him is plainly at the Day of the Lord (vs. 2, chap. 5). The natural flow of the letter Paul wrote if unbroken by verse and chapter divisions, plainly develops the rapture of

4:13-18 into the time called the Day of the Lord (I Thess. 5:1-2).

> "<u>But</u> (note: this word "but" is plainly referring to the rapture
> which was just discussed in the preceding verses) of the times
> and the seasons, brethren, ye have no need that I write unto
> you. For yourselves know perfectly that the day of the Lord
> so cometh as a thief in the night."

6. The comfort that God was going to send destruction upon those
    persecuting the Thessalonian saints at Christ's coming was developed
    starting in 2:16 and enlarged in 5:2-3.

    > "For yourselves know perfectly that the day of the Lord so
    > cometh as a thief in the night. For when they shall say peace
    > and safety; then sudden destruction cometh upon them, as
    > travail upon a woman with child; and they shall not escape."

7. That the wicked would not escape though they dwelt in peace (vs. 3),

    > "For when they shall say Peace and safety; then sudden
    > destruction cometh upon them, as travail upon a woman
    > with child; and they shall not escape."

but the saints <u>would</u> escape and were to watch being comforted by this
hope. How would they escape? By the rapture just before the Day of the
Lord began (Ch. 4:14-18). Ch. 5:9-10 re-emphasizes deliverance from
the day of the Lord.

> "For God hath not appointed us to wrath but to obtain
> salvation by our Lord Jesus Christ who died for us that
> whether we wake or sleep, we should live together with
> Him."

8. With the frailty of the Thessalonian's faith and fear for their lapsing from
    standing for Christ due to persecution, this second letter was written and
    Paul re-emphasized the vengeance of God to come on those who were
    persecuting the earthly church. II Thess. 1:4-9&10

    > "So that we ourselves glory in you in the churches of God for
    > your patience and faith in all your persecutions and tribu-
    > lations that ye endure; which is the manifest token of the
    > righteous judgement of God, for ye may be counted worthy

of the kingdom of God, for which ye also suffer. Seeing it is a righteous thing with God to recompense tribulation to them that trouble you; And to you who are troubled rest with us, when the Lord Jesus shall be revealed from heaven with His mighty angels; In flaming fire taking vengeance on them that know not God, and that obey not the gospel of our Lord Jesus Christ; Who shall be punished with everlasting destruction from the presence of the Lord, and from the glory of His power; When He shall come to be glorified (glorified in our rapture unto Himself) in His saints, (the saints of all ages) and to be admired in all them that believe (because our testimony among you was believed) in that day."

9. Again, the emphasis is that when Christ comes, the saints are going to be glorified in Him (vs. 10) i.e. to receive their glorified bodies at the rapture. This is all contextual.

10. Comfort was also needed to reassure the saints that the Day of the Lord or the day of Christ was not imminent or any moment, i.e. at hand (vs. 1&2, ch. 2).

"Now we beseech you, brethren, by the coming of our Lord Jesus Christ, and by our gathering together unto him, that ye be not soon shaken in mind, or be troubled, neither by spirit, nor by word, nor by letter as from us, as that the day of Christ is at hand."

The reason? Because the Antichrist would <u>first</u> need to be revealed (vs. 3&4).

"Let no man deceive you by any means; for that day shall not come, except there come a falling away <u>first,</u> and that man of sin be revealed, the son of perdition; Who opposeth and exalteth himself above all that is called God, or that is worshipped; so that he as God sitteth in the temple of God, shewing himself that he is God."

11. They also needed to be aware that the Antichrist would be: a) revealed as to his identity to <u>them,</u> b) that they would see him sit in the temple of God proclaiming himself God (both points a real death blow to the pre-trib rapture), c) that the Antichrist would be revealed before the wrath of

God fell, ch. 4&5 of I Thess., d) that the coming of Christ would be after the working and manifestation of Satan in the man of sin. Ch. 2:8&9.

> "And then shall that Wicked be revealed, whom the Lord shall consume with the spirit of His mouth, and shall destroy with the brightness of His coming; Even him WHOSE COMING IS AFTER THE WORKING OF SATAN with all power and signs and lying wonders.

The Biblical truths established in I and II Thessalonians are as follows:

A. The persecuted Christians would be vindicated by Christ's coming to bring vengeance upon the wicked at the Day of the Lord or the Day of Christ

B. That they would escape by the rapture (escape the wrath of the Day of the Lord).

C. That the Day of the Lord could not come until first the Antichrist was revealed and manifested his satanic powers and miracles.

Chapter VII

The Vengeful and Terrible Day of the Lord
Forecasted by Two Cosmic Disturbances Never Before,
Or Never Thereafter Occurring.

Isaiah 13:9-11 - "Behold the day of the Lord cometh, cruel both with wrath and fierce anger, to lay the land desolate; and He shall destroy sinners thereof out of it. For the stars of heaven and the constellations thereof shall not give their light; the sun shall be darkened in His going forth, and the moon shall not cause her light to shine. And I will punish the world for their evil, and the wicked for their iniquity, and I will cause the arrogancy of the proud to cease, and will lay low the haughtiness of the terrible."

Joel 2:1, 10, 31 - "Blow ye the trumpet in Zion, and sound an alarm in my holy mountain; let all the inhabitants of the land tremble, for the day of the Lord cometh, for it is nigh at hand. The earth shall quake before them; the heavens shall tremble, the sun and the moon shall be dark, and the stars shall withdraw their shining. The sun shall be turned into darkness, and the moon into blood, before the great and the terrible day of the Lord come."

Acts 2:20 - "The sun shall be turned into darkness, and the moon into blood, before that great and notable day of the Lord come."

Matthew 24:29 - "Immediately after the tribulation of those days shall the sun be darkened, and the moon shall not give her light, and the stars shall fall from heaven, and the powers of the heavens shall be shaken."

These scriptures plainly, irrefutably, and without any question, establish two special cosmic signs immediately occurring before the vengeful terrible day of the Lord begins, the sun darkening and the moon refusing to give her light and turning to blood. The next statement and scripture should make any honest pre-tribist instantly repudiate his position on a pre-trib rapture.

The Holy Scriptures place the two special cosmic signs occurring AT THE OPENING OF THE SIXTH SEAL IN THE MIDST OF DANIEL'S SEVENTIETH WEEK AND NOT AT THE END OF IT. This concurring with the identical event in Matt. 24:29 proves Matt. 24:29 occurs in the midst of the 70th week and not at the end of it. It then naturally follows that Matt. 24:30, where the tribes of the earth see Christ coming in the clouds of heaven with power and great glory, IS NOT THE SAME EVENT AS REV. 19:11-14 WHERE JESUS COMES <u>WITH</u> HIS SAINTS. THEREFORE IT FOLLOWS THAT THE GATHERING OF THE ELECT FROM THE FOUR WINDS IS NOTHING LESS THAN THE RAPTURE OF THE CHURCH <u>BEFORE</u> THE BEGINNING OF THE TERRIBLE DAY OF THE LORD. Rev. 6:16-17, "...Fall on us, and hide us from the face of Him that sitteth on the throne, and from the wrath of the Lamb. For the great day of His wrath is come; and who shall be able to stand?" Rev. 6:12 irrefutably places the two cosmic disturbances taking place at the opening of the sixth seal. Rev. 6:12 - "And I beheld when he had opened the sixth seal, and, lo, there was a great earthquake; and the <u>SUN BECAME BLACK AS SACKCLOTH OF HAIR, AND THE MOON BECAME AS BLOOD</u>." (What do the ungodly "see" after the opening of the sixth seal? They "see" a) the heavens opening as a scroll is rolled together, b) God the Father sitting on the throne. Where is Jesus - He is at this point <u>off</u> of His throne and coming in the clouds in power and great glory (Matt. 24:30) for the pre-wrath rapture of the church! Jesus at this point comes only in the clouds, and not to the earth, and raptures His saints out before the trumpet and vial judgements are poured out which is what the Day of the Lord is all about punishing the wicked, destroying them out of the land, subduing the earth, and bringing in the millennium. The disciples asked (Matt. 24:3) what would be the sign of His coming. Jesus plainly told them the sign would be the sun darkening and the moon darkening and turning to blood and the stars falling to earth! COMPARING MATT. 24:29-30 TO REV. 6:12-13 IRREFUTABLY PROVES THAT THESE ARE <u>IDENTICAL</u> PROPHECIES OCCURRING AT THE SIXTH SEAL, THIS IS SIMPLY IMPOSSIBLE TO DENY WITHOUT BLASPHEMING THE INSPIRATION OF HOLY SCRIPTURE. The scriptures mean what they say, and say what they mean.

A note on the two witnesses who appear on earth during the seal and trumpet judgements; since it is plain they will witness for 3-1/2 years before being killed, the battle rages over whether they will be here for the first 3-1/2 years or the last 3-1/2 years. The answer is simple! <u>Neither!</u> They appear on earth sometime before the sixth seal is opened in order to prepare the 144,000 Jews for their role in this time period. Malachi 4:5-6 says "Behold, I will send you Elijah the prophet before the coming of the great and dreadful Day of the Lord; and he shall turn the heart of the fathers to the children, and the heart of the children to their fathers, lest I come and smite the earth with a curse." Thus the two witnesses' 3-1/2 years on earth begins sometime during the latter portion or the first 3-1/2 year period (probably about 1 to 1-1/2 years before the 6th seal or so, and extends on into the last 3-1/2 year period probably for about 2 to 2-1/2 years thus totalling 3-1/2 years.

The Latter Day Apostasy and Contributing Elements

There have been many contributing factors in the final form of apostasy which would cause a great falling away from what, by who? From sin by sinners or from righteousness by saints? Certainly the latter. I am listing a number of heresies infiltrating the church, the fundamental soul winning separated church causing sin to abound, the Spirit of God to be quenched and grieved, revival to fail and souls to be lost.

1. Moderate Theology - Attempts to bridge the gap between Biblical soundness and apostates. Billy Graham (though he originally started his ministry Biblically) has done much to promote this bridge as a moderate. The interesting thing to note is once a strong conservative accepts this type theology, moderatism, automatically he has become the same thing. A marriage between the liberals and conservatives cannot take place without first becoming a moderate. (The point is not how much good Graham has done but how much apostasy has been able to flourish because of his moderate stand, and how much more he could have done had he stayed true to fundamentalism (the same with Van Impe!).

2. Pre-tribism - Establishes the Bible as a book to be interpreted in the light as personal theology and preference, and that which is popular as opposed to Biblical soundness.

3. Ruckmanism - Notorious apostate Peter Ruckman is a pied piper of departure from God's Holy Word as is preserved in the original languages. Also, he claims the door of Divine Inspiration is still open, opening the door a) to his heretical advanced revelations, and b) a false stamp of God's approval upon him and all subsequent purported-post biblical relevelations.

4. Hyper-Calvinism - Absolutely kills soul winning fervor and zeal blaming

God (in reality) for souls going to hell because he didn't elect them to be saved. Ignores free moral will in favor of God's sovereignty forcing some to be saved.

5. Charismaticism - Purports to endorse into one body, the body of Christ, all who experience the "heavenly language" under the control of the Holy Ghost (supposedly) irrespective of their doctrine on salvation i.e., Baptists, Church of Christ, Lutheran, Catholic, etc. into one body of supposed brothers and sisters in Christ as long as they speak in their "heavenly language." (It needs to be noted that it is well known that the tongues people do not have the supernatural gift to speak an actual language, but they claim to speak in a heavenly tongue or a language of heaven. What are these heavenly language tongue speakers to do when they finally read their Bible and see they are FORBIDDEN to speak in a HEAVENLY LANGUAGE. Paul plainly said that words spoken in a heavenly tongue or language are forbidden to be spoken or uttered (Read II Cor. 12:4).

6. Prosperity Gospel- I.E. if you are right with God, then your faith will bring you health, wealth and prosperity. Kenneth Copeland ministries as well as others, promote this. This type theology makes God their servant by dictatorial praying and commands for God to do this or that. Those remaining in sickness, disease, and poverty etc. are relegated to living in sin, and lacking in faith.

7. Corrupted Music - The idea to win people by becoming like them has brought gospel rock, contemporary, heavy metal so called "Christian" music into the church. The truth is that only the saving gospel of Christ can change a depraved heart and produce a new life.

8. Lowered Standards - Churches as never before are endorsing or allowing behavior by members in direct violation to Biblical standards. Lodges, secret societies, women dressing like men with short hair and pants, men with long hair like women, attendance of decadent Hollywood films, uncontrolled television, etc. Is this any wonder that apostasy abounds in our churches and they become a breeding ground for immorality, as well as assisting in the creation of a lawless society paving the way for Antichrist?

9. "The Promise Keepers" and all similar movements based on the same theological pedestal. The theological base here is every segment of Christian church, regardless of doctrine is acceptable to Christ, worthy of acceptance and doctrinal credibility, and should all join together under the

banner of seven honorable promises to further strengthen the kingdom of God! (This is inclusive of all so-called Christian churches such as Roman Catholicism which practices idolatry in the worship of the elevated host of the mass, which host supposedly becomes literally the body and blood of our Savior! This is blasphemy and idolatry for which multitudes and multitudes of God's children [non-Roman Christians] were tortured and burnt at the stake for their refusal to accept mass and convert to Roman Catholicism). The "promise keepers" ignore the truth of God's Word in being separate from apostasy and seeks to unify these with God's people! Any person, church, pastor, bible college, etc. who or which endorses this apostate philosophy must be dealt with by: 1) Open rebuke and reproof, 2) Breaking of fellowship with, 3) Marking of those who endorse and promote such apostasy! Granted, the promises have noble intent but are paving the road to hell by good intentions. See "The Promise Keepers" by M.H. Reynolds, P.O. Box 6278, Los Osos, CA 93412 for complete expose which includes Roman Catholic endorsement! If these facts aren't bad enough - now those promoting the promise keepers are calling commitments to these promises as "decisions for Christ!" Is this the new supposed salvation decisions of the apostate church?)

Will the Pre-Trib Rapture Heresy Prevail
Over the Church Until the Rapture?

Unfortunately, I believe that it will for the following reasons:

A)   The pre-trib rapture heresy is so ingrained in the church that it has nearly been elevated in doctrinal status of importance to the level of the virgin birth, or bodily resurrection, etc.

B)   Most pre-tribist pastors readily cold shoulder those of different doctrinal persuasion on the rapture and close their pulpits to them.

C)   Most pre-trib churches today would refuse to consider a pastoral candidate if he is a mid- or post-trib rapturist.

D)   Most pastors are convinced the entire 70th week of Daniel yet to come is, 1) Jewish for Jews only, 2) A time of wrath in its entirety and thus we as Christians are not appointed to wrath but to rapture.

E)   Most pastors are totally closed to reading or studying any literature on a post/mid-trib rapture.

F) Most Christians believe God will not allow His people to suffer such persecution and conflict as comes with the first 4-5 seals of Rev. 6, under the Antichrist, war, famines, and plagues.

G) The scriptures indicated that during the end times the church, rather than fleeing upon the revealing of the Antichrist, will rather be destroyed (Probably due to pre-trib, pre-Antichrist rapture doctrine and therefore waiting to be raptured). Nowhere in scripture is the church said to be able to prevail against the Antichrist by warfare.

H) The Scofield Reference Bible is firmly entrenched in most pre-trib churches. Scofield picked up the pre-trib virus from Darby and his followers. Interestingly, while pastors jealously guard their pulpits (and rightly so) the once divorced, twice married Scofield is preached from these same pulpits (which would not allow a divorced minister to stand in them). To them the Scofield Reference Bible is a final authority. Truly a double standard!

(While I must go on record here as being staunchly opposed to divorce at the same time, should a God called Minister find himself the object of an unjustified divorce he must <u>not</u> lay down the mantle to preach but go <u>on</u> - trusting God to open the doors as He sees fit. While God hates "putting away," He also hates a proud look, lying tongue, etc. (Prov. 6:16) all of which are sins and <u>can</u> be forgiven. Many Pharisaical pastors often relegate divorce to the status as an unforgiveable sin and hold a fellow pastor as "not blameless" when they themselves are <u>not</u> blameless in speech, soulwinning, separation from apostasy and a miriad of other pastoral sins! A pastor (<u>if</u> truly innocent) <u>must</u> fulfill his calling, and continue doing so though he may be <u>crippled</u> by an unjustified divorce. Better to continue the warfare as crippled in battle than to count such a condition as an exit from God's calling! There is no discharge from that warfare! God will hold you accountable to your calling! - <u>Not</u> God first, family second, and church third, but <u>God first</u> and everything second!)

CPSIA information can be obtained at www.ICGtesting.com
Printed in the USA
LVOW101941140613

338670LV00020B/466/P